Lerner SPORTS

ALL-STAR SMACKDOWN

KEVIN DURANT VS. LARRY BIRD

WHO WOULD WIN?

MARGARET J. GOLDSTEIN

Lerner Publications ◆ Minneapolis

Lerner Publications Company
An imprint of Lerner Publishing Group, Inc.
241 First Avenue North
Minneapolis, MN 55401 USA

For reading levels and more information, look up this title at www.lernerbooks.com.

Main body text set in Aptifer Sans LT Pro. Typeface provided by Linotype AG.

Editor: Angel Kidd **Photo Editor:** Angel Kidd

Library of Congress Cataloging-in-Publication Data

Names: Goldstein, Margaret J. author.
Title: Kevin Durant vs. Larry Bird : who would win? / Margaret J. Goldstein.
Other titles: Kevin Durant versus Larry Bird
Description: Minneapolis, MN : Lerner Publishing Group, [2025] | Series: All-star smackdown | Includes bibliographical references and index. | Audience: Ages 7–11 | Audience: Grades 2–3 | Summary: "With multiple championship wins under their belts, Kevin Durant and Larry Bird are two impressive NBA forwards. But who would be victorious in a head-to-head matchup? Read about their careers and decide who's the best!"— Provided by publisher.
Identifiers: LCCN 2024008845 (print) | LCCN 2024008846 (ebook) | ISBN 9798765648247 (library binding) | ISBN 9798765661406 (paperback) | ISBN 9798765653159 (epub)
Subjects: LCSH: Durant, Kevin, 1988-—Juvenile literature. | Bird, Larry 1962- | Basketball players—United States—Biography—Juvenile literature.
Classification: LCC GV884.D868 G65 2025 (print) | LCC GV884.D868 (ebook) | DDC 796.323092—dc23/eng/20240307

LC record available at https://lccn.loc.gov/2024008845
LC ebook record available at https://lccn.loc.gov/2024008846

Manufactured in the United States of America
1-1010827-53382-5/16/2024

TABLE OF CONTENTS

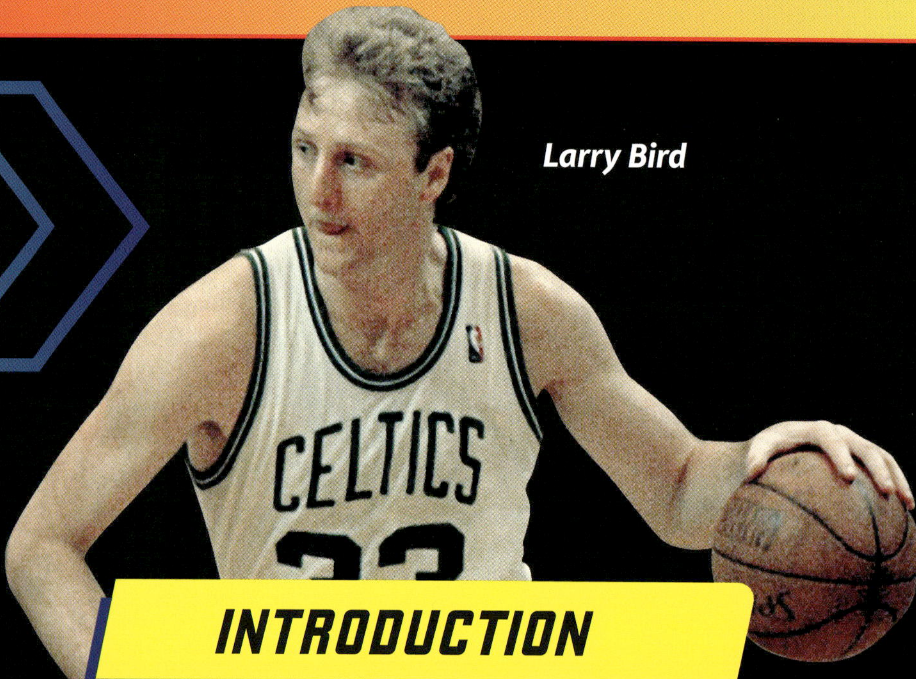

Larry Bird

INTRODUCTION

IN THE CLUTCH

The game between the Boston Celtics and the Los Angeles Lakers was tied 123–123 in overtime. As the clock ticked down to 16 seconds, Celtic Dennis Johnson passed the ball to teammate Larry Bird. In a flash, Bird turned, jumped, and scored. That basket, in Game 4 of the 1984 National Basketball Association (NBA) Finals, put the Celtics up by two.

Fast Facts

- Larry Bird won three NBA championships, in 1981, 1984, and 1986.
- Bird made the All-Defensive Team three times.
- Kevin Durant won two NBA championships, in 2017 and 2018.
- Durant won the NBA scoring title four times.

They scored a few more points before the buzzer sounded. Victory! The whole team had played well, but Bird stood out with 29 points, 21 rebounds, and three steals. The Celtics went on to win the NBA championship.

More than 30 years later, the Golden State Warriors were locked in battle for the 2017 NBA championship. Their opponents were the Cleveland Cavaliers. Cleveland had superstar forward LeBron James. But Golden State had its own big forward: Kevin Durant.

Kevin Durant

In Game 3 of the series, the Cavaliers led 113–111 with just 45 seconds left in the game. That's when Durant grabbed a rebound. He raced down the court and nailed a three-pointer over James's head. The basket helped Golden State win 118–113. The Warriors went on to win the series and become the 2017 NBA champions.

Kevin Durant shoots over Cleveland Cavaliers players during the 2017 NBA Finals.

Larry Bird and Kevin Durant are two of the best forwards ever to play in the NBA. A forward's job is to score baskets. Bird did that job remarkably well. Durant is still playing in the NBA and is one of the league's best scorers. Which athlete is better? Read on and decide for yourself.

Larry Bird tries to score past Los Angeles Lakers star Kareem Abdul-Jabbar in 1984.

CHAPTER 1

Indiana State's Larry Bird (left) plays in the final game of the 1979 men's national college basketball tournament.

NBA-BOUND

Larry Bird grew up in a small town in Indiana called French Lick. He was a star on his high school basketball team. His skill won him a scholarship to play for Indiana University. Indiana had one of the nation's best basketball teams, but Bird felt out of place there. He switched to Indiana State University, a smaller school.

With Bird on the squad, the Indiana State Sycamores became winners. They made it all the way to the 1979

National Collegiate Athletic Association (NCAA) championship game. There, the Sycamores faced the Michigan State Spartans. Bird led his team in scoring, but the Spartans played better. Their star point guard, Earvin "Magic" Johnson, took the team to a 75–64 victory and the NCAA title. With that game, Bird and Johnson began a rivalry that continued in the NBA.

Bird pulls down a rebound during the 1979 NCAA championship game.

After college, Bird joined the Boston Celtics, an NBA team with a losing record. But it wouldn't stay that way for long. In just his second pro season, Bird led his team to the NBA championship. Bird played with Boston his entire career.

Bird (right) holds up his new Boston Celtics jersey with Celtics president Red Auerbach after the team drafted Bird in 1979.

Kevin Durant dribbles the ball during the 2006 McDonald's All-American High School basketball game.

Kevin Durant grew up in Maryland near Washington, DC. He was a standout on youth basketball teams. In high school, he switched schools twice so he could play against tougher opponents.

Many colleges offered him scholarships. He chose the University of Texas. There, he averaged 27.3 points per game. He helped his team reach the second round of the NCAA tournament in 2007. That season he won many honors, including the Naismith College Player of the Year Award.

Durant (left) plays for the University of Texas in 2006.

CONSIDER THIS

Durant starred in the 2012 children's movie *Thunderstruck*. In the film, Durant plays himself, a pro basketball player. Trouble begins when Durant's basketball skills are magically transferred from him to a teenage boy.

Durant felt he was ready for the pros. He entered the NBA Draft in 2007. The Seattle SuperSonics took him with the number two draft pick. Since joining the NBA, Durant has played for five teams: the SuperSonics, Oklahoma City Thunder, Golden State Warriors, Brooklyn Nets, and Phoenix Suns.

Durant talks to reporters after the 2007 NBA Draft.

CHAPTER 2

Bird competed in the 1985 NBA playoffs.

PLAYMAKERS

Larry Bird's 13 seasons in the NBA were filled with amazing moments. They included daring steals, clutch baskets, and thundering dunks.

An important moment came in March 1985 when Bird set the Celtics single-game scoring record with 60 points against the Atlanta Hawks. As of 2024, the record is still 60 and is held by both Bird and Jayson Tatum.

Another big game for Bird came on February 14, 1986. Bird scored 47 points against the Portland Trail Blazers. He shot the game-winning basket with three seconds left in overtime.

What made this moment extra special was that the right-handed Bird made many of those points shooting with his left hand. Why did he use the left? He joked to a reporter that he was saving his right hand for an upcoming game against the Los Angeles Lakers, Magic Johnson's team. In that game Boston beat the Lakers 105–99.

Bird prepares to shoot as James Worthy (left) and Magic Johnson (right) attempt to stop him in a 1986 game.

Bird (right) passes to a teammate during a 1987 NBA Eastern Conference finals game.

Bird was a team player. Rather than always taking a shot, he passed off to teammates so they could score. One famous example came in Game 5 of the 1987 NBA Eastern Conference finals, against the Detroit Pistons.

With only five seconds left in the game, Boston trailed by one point. A Piston tried to pass, but Bird swooped in and stole the ball. He quickly sent it off to teammate Dennis Johnson, who made the game-winning basket. The final score was 108–107.

Kevin Durant is famous for scoring and making clutch plays. He displayed both these talents on March 21, 2014. Durant's team, the Oklahoma Thunder, faced the Toronto Raptors. The game was in double overtime, with just seconds remaining. Toronto led 118–116, but Kevin Durant did not back down. He shot the game-winning three-pointer with just 1.7 seconds left. What's more, he scored a sky-high 51 points in the game.

Durant prepares to shoot a free throw on March 21, 2014.

In 2016, Durant joined the Golden State Warriors. With Durant and point guard Stephen Curry, the team was nearly unstoppable. They shut down LeBron James and the Cleveland Cavaliers to win the 2017 NBA championship.

A year later, Golden State faced Cleveland for the championship. In Game 3, several Warriors struggled. In the fourth quarter, the lead switched back and forth. Both teams wanted the win.

Durant dribbles the ball past Cleveland Cavaliers defender Tristan Thompson during Game 5 of the 2017 NBA Finals.

CONSIDER THIS

Both Bird and Durant have played basketball in the Olympics. Bird played in 1992, alongside Magic Johnson, Michael Jordan, and other greats. This US "Dream Team" won the gold medal. Fans are excited to see Durant compete for a fourth gold medal at the 2024 Olympics in Paris, France.

With 50 seconds left in the game, Durant hit a three-pointer to put Golden State up by six. Thanks to Durant's 43 points, the Warriors won. They went on to win the championship.

San Antonio Spurs point guard Dejounte Murray (left) has his shot blocked by Durant (right) during a 2017 game.

Durant can be a monster on defense. In one 2017 game, San Antonio Spurs point guard Dejounte Murray was racing down the court toward an easy score. Durant made sure that didn't happen. He caught up with Murray, jumped, and blocked the shot. Twice! First, he blocked the ball with his right hand. It bounced off the backboard, where Durant hit it again with his left.

CHAPTER 3

Bird hangs on the rim as he slams the ball through the hoop during the 1984 NBA Finals.

CAREER HIGHLIGHTS

Larry Bird led the Boston Celtics to the NBA Finals five times. He won the championship three times, in 1981, 1984, and 1986. His three-point shooting was legendary. In the NBA All-Star Three-Point Contest, players compete to see who can make the most three-pointers in one minute. Bird won the contest three years in a row.

Bird was more than just a scorer. He made the NBA All-Defensive Team three times. And he was the ultimate team player. He saw the big picture of which teammates were in a position to score and where he needed to pass the ball.

The league honored his greatness. He was a three-time NBA Most Valuable Player (MVP) and a 12-time All-Star. During his 13 years in the NBA, he scored 21,791 points. A member of the NBA Hall of Fame, Bird is nicknamed Larry Legend.

Bird (left) shakes hands with the president of the Basketball Hall of Fame as Bird becomes a member of the Hall of Fame in 2010.

CONSIDER THIS

Larry Bird's name is famous beyond basketball. The social media company Twitter (which became X) started in 2006. Its logo was a blue bird. Twitter cofounder Biz Stone, who grew up watching the Boston Celtics, called the logo Larry the Bird.

Kevin Durant is also an NBA legend. He's won two NBA championships and was named finals MVP twice. He was the NBA MVP in 2014 and has been named to 14 NBA All-Star teams.

Durant shoots in the 2024 All-Star Game.

Durant is a fierce shot blocker, rebounder, and defender. But he is best known for getting the ball into the basket. He has led the league in points scored per game four times. He posted his highest-scoring game on April 2, 2022, when he was a Brooklyn Net. In that game, he scored 55 points against the Atlanta Hawks. By 2024, after almost two decades in the NBA, Durant was still considered one of its greats.

Durant leaps for the basket on April 2, 2022.

CHAPTER 4

Bird holds the ball in the 1984 NBA playoffs.

AND THE WINNER IS

Who's the better forward—Larry Bird or Kevin Durant? We can look at their records and watch video of their games to determine who is the better player.

Larry Bird couldn't jump as high or run as fast as Kevin Durant. But he used his great knowledge of the game to outsmart opponents. He was also a tremendous team player. He knew when it was best to pass the ball and when it was best to shoot it himself. He pushed himself and his team to play better. He was also a great defensive player. He made the NBA All-Defensive Team three times. As of 2024, Durant has never made that team.

Durant dunks for the Phoenix Suns during a 2024 NBA game.

At 6 feet 11 (2.1 m) and 240 pounds (109 kg), Durant is big and powerful. He doesn't just dunk the ball. He slams it through the net. When he's fighting for a rebound, he puts his whole body into it. He uses his big wingspan to keep the ball from defenders and to score over their heads. When it comes to scoring, Durant tops Bird. By the end of the 2023–2024 regular season, Durant had averaged 27.3 points per game for his career. Bird's average was 24.3 points per game.

Both men rank among the greatest forwards of all time. But Bird was the better all-around player, so he wins this smackdown. You might have a different opinion. Which do you think is the better player and why?

Durant uses his long wingspan to block Spain's Ricky Rubio during the 2020 Summer Olympics.

Bird talks to a reporter before a game in the 1980s.

SMACKDOWN BREAKDOWN

LARRY BIRD

Date of birth: December 7, 1956
Height: 6 feet 9 (2.1 m)
NBA championships: 3
NBA MVP awards: 3
All-Star Games: 12

Stats are accurate through the 2023–2024 NBA regular season.

KEVIN DURANT

Date of birth: September 29, 1988
Height: 6 feet 11 (2.1 m)
NBA championships: 2
NBA MVP awards: 1
All-Star Games: 14

GLOSSARY

All-Defensive Team: a group chosen as the best defensive players in basketball each year

All-Star: an athlete chosen as the best in their position from all the teams in a league

clutch: successful in important moments and games

draft: when teams take turns choosing new players

dunk: a shot in which a player jumps above the rim and pushes the ball down through the net

forward: a player who usually plays near the basket

point guard: a player who leads a basketball team on offense

rebound: grabbing and controlling the ball after a missed shot

rivalry: when a player or team tries to defeat or be more successful than another

scholarship: money given to a student to help pay for school

wingspan: the distance from the right middle fingertip to the left middle fingertip with arms outstretched

LEARN MORE

Fun Basketball Facts for Kids
https://www.sciencekids.co.nz/sciencefacts/sports/basketball.html

Kjartansson, Kjartan Atli. *Legends of the NBA*. New York: Abbeville Kids, 2022.

Larry Bird
https://academickids.com/encyclopedia/index.php/Larry_Bird

Levit, Joe. *Meet Kevin Durant*. Minneapolis: Lerner Publications, 2023.

Stabler, David. *Inside the Boston Celtics*. Minneapolis: Lerner Publications, 2023.

20 Fun Basketball Facts for Kids
https://www.growingplay.com/2023/03/20-fun-basketball-facts-for-kids/

INDEX

PHOTO ACKNOWLEDGMENTS

Image credits: AP Photo/Elise Amendola, p. 4; AP Photo/Marcio Jose Sanchez, p. 5; AP Photo/Carlos Avila Gonzalez/San Francisco Chronicle, p. 6; AP Photo/Doug Pizac, p. 7; AP Photo, pp. 8–10, 20; AP Photo/Denis Poroy, p. 11; AP Photo/Deborah Cannon, p. 12; AP Photo/Jason DeCrow, p. 13; AP Photo/Peter Southwick, p. 14; Rick Stewart/Allsport/Getty Images, p. 15; AP Photo/Dave Tenenbaum, p. 16; Rick Madonik/Toronto Star/Getty Images, p. 17; AP Photo/Scott Strazzante/San Francisco Chronicle, p. 18; AP Photo/Eric Gay, p. 19; AP Photo/Mark J. Terrill, p. 21; AP Photo/Darron Cummings, p. 22; AP Photo/Hakim Wright Sr., p. 23; AP Photo/Steve Pyle, p. 24; AP Photo/Nick Wass, p. 25; AP Photo/Charlie Neibergall, p. 26; AP Photo/John W. McDonough/Icon Sportswire, pp. 27–28; AP Photo/Matt Slocum, p. 29.

Cover: AP Photo/Charles Krupa; AP Photo/Rick Scuteri.